"Strange Street? Where is that?"
says Ben.

"I'll show you," says Sam.
She presses the magic button.

WHOOOSH!

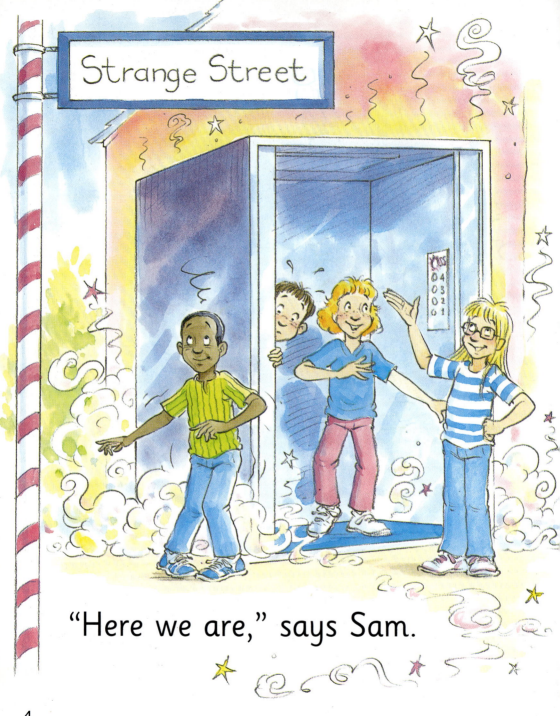

"Here we are," says Sam.

Sam, Ben, Mouse and Jojo walk along the street.

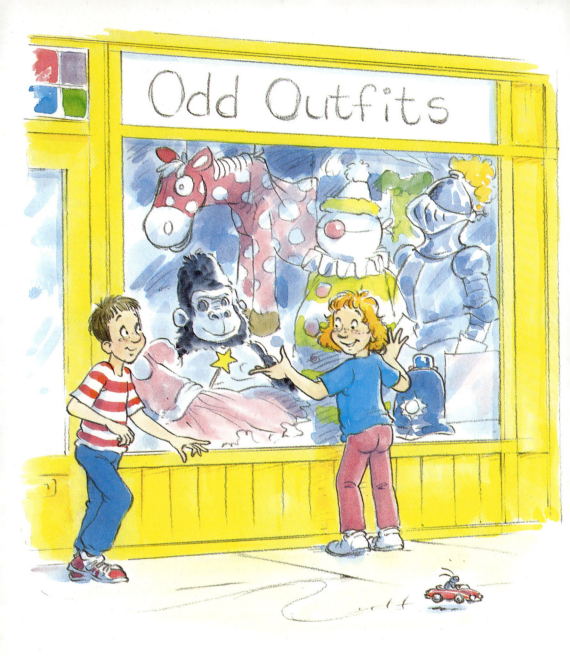

"I want to go in there," says Jojo.

"This is fun!" says Ben.

Mouse goes into the magic shop.

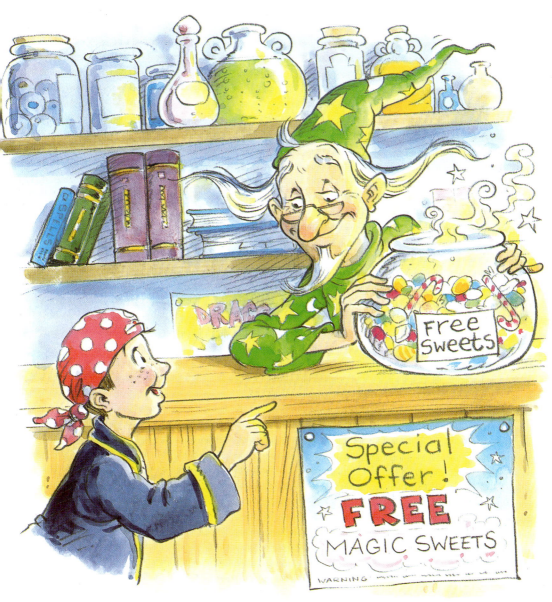

"Some sweets, please," says
Mouse.

"They are magic sweets," says the
old man.

"I like magic sweets," says Mouse.

Oh no, Mouse is a mouse!

"We must take him home,"
says Ben.

They run to the lift.

"That was strange," says Ben.

"Too strange!" says Mouse.